Managing Money

...ney
...nsumer

...mons

...	2
...	4
...ause	
...	9
...	10
...ata	15
...s	16
...sions	19
...	20
...	21
...	22
...	23
Index	24

Millmark
EDUCATION

Please return materials on time

HIGHLINE COMMUNITY COLLEGE LIBRARY
P.O. BOX 98000
DES MOINES, WA 98198-9800

WITHDRAWN
Highline College Library

DEMCO

DEVELOP LANGUAGE

People are **consumers**. They buy and use many kinds of **goods** and **services**.

Look at the photographs. Discuss what they show about people as consumers. Ask and answer questions like these:

What goods are people buying?
What services are they buying?
Why do you think these consumers are buying these goods and services?
Which are items that they want?
Which are items that they need?

As a consumer, what kinds of goods and services do you buy?

consumers – people who buy and use goods or services
goods – items that people make
services – work that people do for others

going on a trip

buying ice cream

shopping at a street fair

having a dentist check your teeth

CHAPTER 1

goods

services

Using Money Wisely

Most people have some **income**. Income comes from different sources. People may earn money by working. They may receive money as gifts. They may earn money from their **investments**.

Most people spend some of their income. They are consumers. They buy and use goods, such as shampoo, food, and shoes. They buy and use services, such as the work of doctors, hair stylists, and private music teachers.

Some goods and services are **needs** and some are **wants**. Needs are goods and services that people must have to survive. Housing and food are needs. Wants are goods and services that people would like to have but do not need. Video games are wants.

income – money earned by working or received from another source

investments – the use of money in a way that is intended to earn more money over time

needs – goods and services that a person must have to survive

wants – goods or services that a person would like to have but doesn't need

Managing Your Money: Be a Wise Consumer

Planning a **budget** helps people make wise decisions about spending and saving their money. People can begin a budget by writing down their income.

Next, **expenses**, or the money paid for goods and services, are listed. Expenses that are needs should be listed first. A budget should also include some money for savings or investments.

> **budget** – a plan for making good decisions about income, spending, and saving
>
> **expenses** – money spent on goods and services

Perry's Monthly Budget

Income		Expenses	
part-time job	$80	lunches	$60
money from parents	$40	school club fees	$15
		savings	$30
total	$120	total	$105

▲ Perry earns $80 each month and receives $40 from his parents. His expenses are $105, including savings of $30. Perry has $15 left to spend on wants, to save, or to invest.

KEY IDEA Budgets help people make wise decisions about money.

Chapter 1: Using Money Wisely

Setting Goals

Setting goals can help a person plan a budget. Short-term goals can be achieved over a short period of time. Guitar lessons or concert tickets might be short-term goals for a budget. Long-term goals take more time to achieve. Going to college, buying a car, or traveling to another country are examples of long-term goals.

Setting goals for saving money and investing is also important. Some people **deposit** money in a **savings account** each month. A bank pays **interest** on the money in a savings account. So money in a savings account earns interest and increases in value.

deposit – put money into a bank account

savings account – a bank account that pays interest on the money put into it

interest – a payment for the use of money; usually a percentage of the total amount

▼ Going to college is a long-term goal. Saving money will help a person reach this goal.

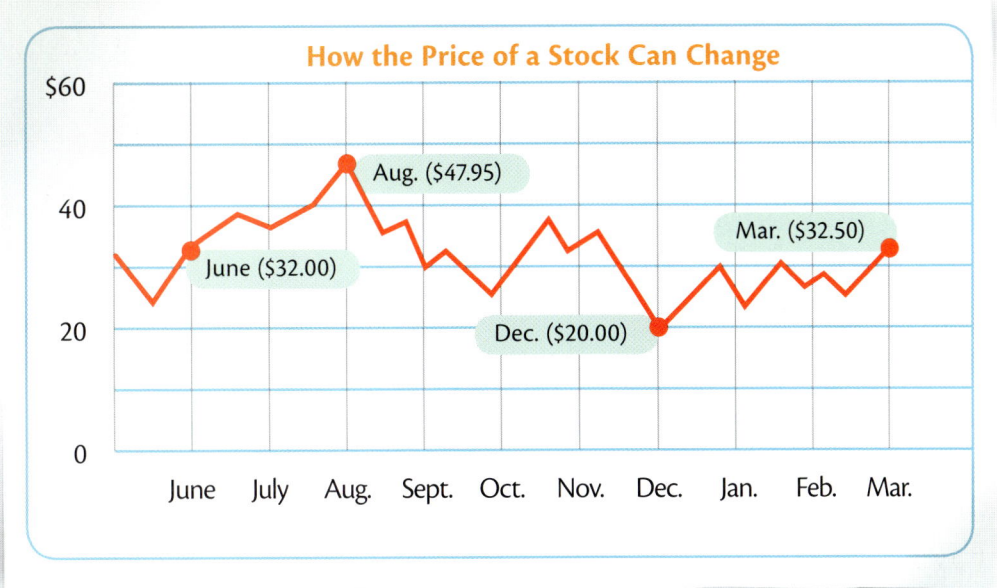

A savings account at a bank is a safe investment because the United States (U.S.) government guarantees the money that a person deposits. A certificate of deposit (CD) is also guaranteed by the U.S. government.

A CD usually earns a higher rate of interest than a savings account. But a CD requires that the money be left in that account for a period of time. If a person **withdraws** money during this period, the bank will charge a **fee**.

Some investments have more **risk** than others. For example, **stocks** have more risk. A stock is a small share of ownership in a company. The price of a stock can rise and fall. People may have to sell a stock for less money than they paid to buy it.

withdraws – takes money out of an account

fee – money that must be paid for a service

risk – the chance of loss

stocks – shares of ownership in a company

KEY IDEAS Saving and investing money can help people reach their goals. Some investments have more risk than others.

Chapter 1: Using Money Wisely

Borrowing Money

Sometimes people cannot save and invest enough money to reach their long-term goals. Some goals, such as buying a house, are expensive. To achieve those goals, people may **borrow** money. They may take out a **loan** from a bank or another **lender**.

Borrowing costs money, because a lender charges interest on the loan. The borrower usually makes a monthly payment over a period of time. Part of the monthly payment is interest on the amount of money owed.

borrow – take money from a person or a bank with the understanding that it will be repaid

loan – the amount of money borrowed

lender – person or bank lending money

KEY IDEAS Sometimes people need to borrow money. Loans cost money because they must be repaid with interest.

YOUR TURN

ANALYZE CAUSE AND EFFECT

A cause is the reason an event happens. An effect is the result of the event. Sometimes one event can have several effects. Create a chart like the one below and add at least one effect. Think of other examples of causes, events, and effects.

Cause →	Event →	Effects
I want to have money for _____.	I decide to follow a budget.	

MAKE CONNECTIONS

Think of one of your short-term goals. What is something you would like to have or do within three months? Then figure out the cost of reaching this goal. Discuss how much you would have to save each month in order to reach your goal.

USE THE LANGUAGE OF SOCIAL STUDIES

What is a consumer?

A consumer is a person who buys and uses goods and services.

Chapter 1: Using Money Wisely

CHAPTER 2

Buyer Beware

Planning a budget, saving money every month, setting short- and long-term goals, and being careful about borrowing money are important steps in making good decisions about money. But many decisions about money have hidden costs. Consumers must be careful to avoid spending more money than they had planned.

By The Way...

More than two thousand years ago in ancient Rome, people were warned, "Caveat emptor." This Latin saying means, "Let the buyer beware." In other words, protecting yourself and your money is your responsibility.

When people borrow money, they take on **debt**. They have to pay back the money they have borrowed and the interest.

People may also take on debt when they use a **credit card** to pay for goods and services. Credit card companies charge interest on the amount of money owed. If a person pays the entire amount each month, no interest is charged. But if the person pays only part of the amount, interest will be charged on the rest.

debt – something that is owed

credit card – a card that people use to charge their expenses and pay for them later

Kimberley bought a new coat for $200.00 on a credit card. The credit card had an interest rate of 12%. She thought that she could pay off the credit card in six months. Her total cost for the coat would be about $212.00.

But Kimberley didn't make the first payment. The company added a fee of $25 for the missed payment and increased her interest rate to 18%. So Kimberley's coat will now cost at least $260. If she misses other payments, or pays late, the total cost will be even more. Kimberley's $200 coat will cost much more than she had planned to spend.

Chapter 2: Buyer Beware

Advertising and Consumer Fraud

Companies advertise their products everywhere—on television and radio, as well as in newspapers and magazines. This is a way for consumers to get information about products. But some advertisements, or ads, can be misleading. Be careful of ads that promise too much. Remember this advice: "If it sounds too good to be true, it probably is."

A **fraud** is a plan to cheat people or get their money dishonestly. "Bait-and-switch" is one kind of fraud. A store advertises an item, such as a TV, at a low price. When a person goes to the store, there are no TVs at that price. Only more expensive TVs are available. The store tries to sell the person a more expensive TV or other item.

Even when there is no fraud, think carefully about ads. The goal of an ad that says "20% off!" is to get you to visit a store. Once inside, you are likely to look at and buy items that are not on sale!

> **fraud** – a plan to cheat people or get their money dishonestly

▶ Some ads bring people into a store by promising bargains that do not really exist.

Explore Language

Word Parts

dis- = not
dishonest = not honest

Many consumer frauds involve advertising and sales on the Internet, on television, or over the telephone.

Some ads say, "Make just a few easy payments." Ads like this often have hidden fees, such as a **shipping and handling fee** or other charges.

Whenever you buy something on the Internet or over the phone, make sure that you are aware of all the charges. Be sure to ask if the item can be returned for a **refund**.

shipping and handling fee – money that a company charges to send an item to the buyer

refund – getting back the money paid for a product

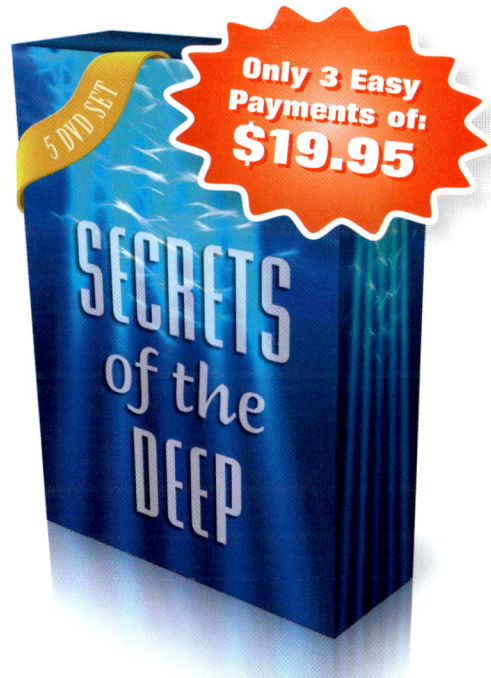

Michael saw an ad on TV for some DVDs that he wanted. The price looked good — only three monthly payments of $19.95. The DVDs would cost about $50.00 at the local store, but he didn't have $50.00 and he wanted the DVDs right away. If he bought them through the TV ad, he could make the payments from the money he earned at his part-time job.

But when Michael called, he found out that each payment had a shipping and handling fee of $7.00. So his total cost would be $79.85! He made a wise decision. He decided to save his money and buy the DVDs in three months.

KEY IDEA Wise consumers are careful about the costs of interest and hidden fees.

Chapter 2: Buyer Beware

Identity Theft

You should always be careful about phone calls and e-mails from people or companies that you do not know. Never give them personal information such as your name, address, or telephone number.

Sometimes dishonest people will try to steal someone else's personal information. They find a way to get into a person's bank and credit card accounts online. Using that person's information, they buy expensive items or take money from bank accounts. This kind of fraud is called identity theft. To prevent identity theft, you must protect your personal information.

Be careful of people who ask for information or try to sell you something over the telephone.

KEY IDEAS Frauds frequently take place on the Internet or over the phone. Wise consumers protect their personal information.

YOUR TURN

INTERPRET DATA

Credit card fees, charges, and interest rates vary from company to company. Interpret the data in the chart to answer the questions.

Fees	Credit Card A	Credit Card B
Late payment fee	$15 on amounts less than $100 $30 on amounts over $100	$15 on amounts less than $250 $35 on amounts over $250
Interest rate	14.99% per year	21.99% per year

1. If you owe $249 and pay late, what fee will you be charged by Credit Card A? by Credit Card B?

2. Which card has a lower interest rate?

MAKE CONNECTIONS

Make a poster that tells how consumers can protect themselves from fraud. Share it with your family. Discuss how you can keep personal information safe.

STRATEGY FOCUS

Determine Importance

Look at this chapter again. What are the most important ideas? What text features help you find the important ideas?

Chapter 2: Buyer Beware

CHAPTER 3

Making Good Decisions

Wise consumers plan budgets and follow them. They make decisions to save and invest their money to help them meet their goals. They watch out for frauds. And they are careful to figure out the total cost of everything they buy.

For most people, money is a limited **resource**. People don't have enough money for all of their needs and wants. This means that people have to make decisions about earning, spending, and saving. This often involves making a trade-off, or giving up something in order to get something else. The trade-off is the **opportunity cost**.

resource – what people use to do something or get something

opportunity cost – the cost of what a person must give up by choosing one thing over another

For example, Sheri usually works part-time during the summer at a food store. She earns about $400 each summer. This summer she is thinking about volunteering at a camp for hearing-impaired children.

The charts show the decisions that she can make and the opportunity cost of each.

If Sheri decides to…	her opportunity cost will be…
work for the summer and earn $400	working with children at the camp.
volunteer at a camp	earning $400 during the summer.

Sheri talked with the manager at the food store and with the director at the camp. She can now make a different decision.

If Sheri decides to…	her opportunity cost will be…
work one month this summer and earn $200; and, volunteer at a camp for one month	working at the camp for one month; and earning $200 during the summer.

SHARE IDEAS What should Sheri do? Which decision would you make? **Discuss** with a partner.

KEY IDEA Understanding opportunity costs helps a person make good decisions about earning, spending, saving, and investing.

Chapter 3: Making Good Decisions

The Wise Consumer's Checklist

Making good decisions about money is important! These questions will help you make decisions as a consumer about spending, borrowing, saving, and investing.

Spending

- Have I paid for all the goods and services I need?
- Is this item a need or a want?
- What is the opportunity cost of buying this item?
- Should I pay with cash or use a credit card?
- Is my personal information safe?

Borrowing and Credit Cards

- What is the interest rate?
- With interest, what will this item really cost me?
- Will I be able to make the payments on time each month?
- If I save before I buy this item, will I avoid borrowing?

Saving and Investing

- Is my account earning the best interest rate?
- Will I pay a fee if I withdraw money?
- How much risk does this investment have?

KEY IDEA Wise consumers ask questions before they make decisions about their money.

YOUR TURN

MAKE DECISIONS

Wise consumers make careful decisions about what they buy. Think of an item that you would like to buy. What questions should you ask before you decide to buy? Make a chart like the one below. Add your questions and answers. Discuss your chart with a partner.

What do I want to buy?	
What questions should I ask myself?	My answers
• Do I need this item now?	

MAKE CONNECTIONS

When people plan their budgets, they often include money for sharing or giving. They might support groups that help children or the environment. What organizations would you like to give money to? Make a list with a partner.

EXPAND VOCABULARY

The word **deposit** can be used as a verb that means "to put money into a bank account." It can also be used as a noun.

> He **deposited** $100 in his account.
> His **deposit** was $100.

Find other words in this book that can be used as verbs and nouns. Write sentences to show the different meanings of each word.

CAREER EXPLORATIONS

Safety Inspectors

Consumers buy many different products every year. Safety inspectors make sure that products are safe for people to use. Safety inspectors can work for the government or for other organizations. They usually work with one type of product.

- Look at the chart. Think about the different jobs.

- What area of safety inspection would you choose? Explain why.

Area	What would you do?	What classes can help you prepare for this career?
Food safety	• visit farms, stores, or restaurants • make sure that foods are clean, fresh, and will not cause illness	biology, food safety
Consumer product safety	• visit factories or work in a lab • test products to make sure that they work and that they will not hurt anyone	chemistry, physical science, engineering
Building safety	• visit homes, office buildings • inspect parts of buildings • write reports about any safety problems	math, physical science, engineering

USE LANGUAGE TO EXPLAIN

Examples that Explain

One way to explain an idea is to give an example. Sometimes the example tells what could happen in real life. When people read it, they can imagine what is happening. Then they can better understand the idea.

EXAMPLE

> Some ads do not tell you everything you need to know about buying a product. For example, Peter saw an ad for TVs. The ad said he could buy a TV now and pay for it in one year. So Peter went to the store. At the store, he found out that he would be charged 2% interest every month until he paid for the TV.

Talk About It

With a partner, reread pages 11 and 13. Take turns explaining how the examples relate to the advice on each page.

Write an Explanation

Choose one of the frauds or hidden charges you read about in Chapter 2.

- Describe the fraud or hidden charge.
- Then give an example of what could happen in real life. Explain what happens to one person who is tricked by the fraud.

Words You Can Use	
ad	fraud
bait-and-switch	interest
credit	payment
fee	

SOCIAL STUDIES AROUND YOU

The Cost of Credit

In September, George bought a used car. The car cost $800. He paid for the car with a credit card. The card has an interest rate of 10%. George must decide how much he will pay each month.

Use the information in the table to answer the questions below.

Payment Options for $800 at 10% Interest			
	Option A	Option B	Option C
Amount that George pays each month	$25	$50	$100
Number of months it will take to repay	38 months	18 months	9 months
Amount of interest that George will pay	$134	$62	$31

1. If George chooses Option A, about how much will he pay in total for the car?

2. George begins making payments in October 2010. If he chooses Option B, when will he finish paying for the car?

3. If George decides to pay $200 per month, how many months will it take him to pay for the car? Will he still have to pay interest?

Managing Your Money: Be a Wise Consumer

Key Words

budget (budgets) a plan for making good decisions about money
A **budget** includes some money for savings.

consumer (consumers) someone who buys and uses goods or services
Consumers should check prices carefully when they shop.

debt (debts) something that is owed
He had a large **debt** because he bought too many things with his credit card.

expense (expenses) money spent on a good or a service
She listed all of her **expenses** in her budget.

fraud (frauds) a plan to cheat people or get their money dishonestly
Many **frauds** involve the Internet.

good (goods) an item that people make
Goods are things that you buy, such as food, clothing, and games.

income money earned by working or received from another source
Tyler's **income** came from mowing lawns.

interest a payment for the use of money; usually a percentage of the total amount
Savings accounts earn **interest**.

investment (investments) the use of money in a way that is intended to earn more money over time
Certificates of deposit are a safe **investment**.

loan (loans) the amount of money borrowed
Ana took out a **loan** to pay for college.

opportunity cost (opportunity costs) the cost of what a person gives up by choosing one thing over another
If you take a trip, one **opportunity cost** is the money you could have earned by staying home.

risk (risks) the chance of loss
Buying stocks has **risk** because the price might go down after you buy them.

service (services) work that people do for others
Healthcare workers are paid for their **services**, such as giving medical care in hospitals.

Index

borrow 8, 10–11, 18
budget 5–6, 9, 10, 16, 19
consumer 2–3, 4, 9, 10, 12–13, 15, 16, 18, 19, 20
credit card 11, 14, 15, 18, 22
debt 11
deposit 6–7, 19
earn 4–7, 13, 16–17
expense 5, 11
fee 5, 7, 11, 13, 15, 18, 21
fraud 12–14, 15, 16, 21

good 2–3, 4–5, 9, 11, 18
income 4–5
interest 6–8, 11, 13, 15, 18, 21, 22
investment 4–5, 7, 18
lender 8
loan 8
need 2–3, 4–5, 8, 16, 18, 19, 21
opportunity cost 16–18

refund 13
resource 16
risk 7, 18
save 8–9, 13, 16, 18
savings account 6
service 2–3, 4–5, 11, 18
spend 4–5, 10–11, 16, 18
stock 7
want 4–5, 16, 18
withdraw 7, 18

MILLMARK EDUCATION CORPORATION
Ericka Markman, President and CEO; Karen Peratt, VP, Editorial Director; Lisa Bingen, VP, Marketing; Dave Willette, VP, Sales; Rachel L. Moir, VP, Operations and Production; Shelby Alinsky, Associate Editor; Ana Nuncio, Language Editor; Hanneman Productions, Photo Research; Arleen Nakama, Technology Projects

PROGRAM AUTHORS
Mary Hawley, Program Author, Instructional Design
Peggy Altoff, Program Author, Social Studies

STUDENT BOOK DEVELOPMENT Gare Thompson Associates, Inc.

BOOK DESIGN Steve Curtis Design

TECHNOLOGY Six Red Marbles

CONTENT REVIEWER
Margit McGuire, PhD, Program Director and Professor of Teacher Education, Seattle University, Seattle, WA

PROGRAM ADVISORS
Scott K. Baker, PhD, Pacific Institutes for Research, Eugene, OR
Carla C. Johnson, EdD, University of Toledo, Toledo, OH
Margit McGuire, PhD, Seattle University, Seattle, WA
Donna Ogle, EdD, National-Louis University, Chicago, IL
Betty Ansin Smallwood, PhD, Center for Applied Linguistics, Washington, DC
Gail Thompson, PhD, Claremont Graduate University, Claremont, CA
Emma Violand-Sánchez, EdD, Arlington Public Schools, Arlington, VA (retired)

PHOTO CREDITS Cover ©REUTERS/John C. Hillery; IFC and 15a ©David Safanda/iStockphoto.com; 1a ©Mario Savola/Shutterstock; 2a ©Robert Llewellyn/agefotostock; 2b ©Timur Kulgarin/Shutterstock; 2-3a ©Jeff Greenberg/Photo Edit; 3a, 3c, 17a ©Michael Newman/Photo Edit; 3b ©Thomas M Perkins/Shutterstock; 4a ©Yanta/Shutterstock; 4b ©vario images GmbH & Co.KG/Alamy; 5a ©Graca Victoria/Shutterstock; 6a ©Dennis MacDonald/Photo Edit; 7a Steve Curtis Design; 8a ©eugeniophoto/iStockphoto; 9a and 9b Photos by Ken Karp; 10a ©Lebrecht Music and Arts Photo Library/Alamy; 11a ©Karkas/Shutterstock; 12a ©Tony Freeman/Photo Edit; 13a ©Alperium/Shutterstock; 13b ©Alhovik/Shutterstock; 14a ©Angela Hampton Picture Library/Alamy; 16a ©Bob Daemmrich/Photo Edit; 18a ©Daniel Kàsler/Shutterstock; 20a ©Gabe Palmer/Alamy; 24a ©Stuart Pearce/agefotostock

Copyright ©2009 Millmark Education Corporation

All rights reserved. Reproduction of the whole or any part of the contents without written permission from the publisher is prohibited. Millmark Education and ConceptLinks are registered trademarks of Millmark Education Corporation.

Published by Millmark Education Corporation
PO Box 30239
Bethesda, MD 20824

ISBN-13: 978-1-4334-0657-7

Printed in the USA

10 9 8 7 6 5 4 3 2 1

Managing Your Money: Be a Wise Consumer